For Better or For Worse

Simran Chandiramani

Presentation by *BookLeaf Publishing*

Web: www.bookleafpub.com

E-mail: info@bookleafpub.com

ISBN: 978-93-95784-46-7

First edition 2022

DEDICATION

To everyone mentioned in this book, thank you
for helping me get to this version of myself -
for better or for worse.

ACKNOWLEDGEMENT

Firstly, I want to acknowledge and thank Book Leaf Publishing for making this all possible! The Write Angle writing challenge has made one of my dreams into reality, and I encourage all other Canadian poets to apply!

Thank you to all my friends who have always believed in me and who made me feel like I was enough.

Lastly, thank you to my family for always making me feel seen and encouraged.

To A.C.

Fire and water shouldn't work, but with us, it does.
Since day one, you've had your eyes set on the stars, mine more down towards earth.
You give a light, fueling you and others, as if you were one of the glowing dots in the night sky yourself.
That light is you, and it will burn on for eons to come.

To A.C. (M)

2

Orange sunlight flows into the room.
Something in the air smells like ripe cranberries.
Papers of scribbles and lines clutched in my
hands, and a soft smile tugs at your lips.
You are my earliest, clear memory.
At that moment, bliss was holding our hands.
I've never truly believed in fate, but our souls
are tied in all worlds.

To R.C.

3

The open window illuminates the silver game
pieces scattered across the board.
Roll the dice and land on chance.
Go back three spaces.
It's your turn. You pass go and get $100.
The game goes on. We keep going forward and
back, occasionally landing on free parking.
When all is done we leave the game,
looking back, sometimes fondly, sometimes not.
But I'm always happy to play the game with
you.

To T. & S.

Summer walks and lazy naps.
No words ever spoken, yet you know me better
than most.
Cold noses and warm hearts.
No words could ever match up, but
you are my unconditional.

To T.D.

In you, I found my moon cascading its glow
across the obsidian night sky.
Dark clouds are no match as you clear a path to
Neverland.
A chain of yellow lilies, twinkling like stardust,
ties our hearts together.
We were
always
meant to find each other, in this world and the
next.
How can something so precious bloom in such
an upside-down world?
Take me to the place that lies second star to the
right and straight on till morning.

To F.Y.

At the end of a long day, you are my pillow.
I can rest with you. No fuss, just warmth.
There was never a question when it came to you.
We were trapped in this illusory gallery together,
but you made the colours shine brighter, made
the blurs turn into shapes.
With you, the night quickly fades away to the
early pastel light of dawn.
I've always preferred sunrises to sunsets.

To T.S.

This world is filled with puzzle pieces.
Yours were the first who fit with mine.
Since then, my puzzle has gotten bigger, and so
has yours.
Spreading and stretching, but never quite losing
that first piece amongst this chaotic art
we've created.
After all these years, I would do it all again if
you were my first resting place.

To A.N.

"I hate you."
Our story started with these three words.
Chapters go by while something much different
grows.
Words meld along with souls.
I will never put this book down.
When we're together, all I see is
yellow.

To N.A.

On the rocky beach, you were my lighthouse.
A familiar shape in the otherwise tangled mess.
When the morning came - and the waves
calmed,
your light
still made all the difference.
You gave the sun competition when it was at its
highest peak.

To K.K.

You are a castle built high enough to reach the
sparkling sun.
Your countless walls never seem to crumble.
Tapestries show thorns, but roses prevail in my
mind.
Hung mirrors reveal the truth.
You were my shelter, and you fought off their
armies.
When the cracks show, ivy hides your scars, but
I will always be there with mortar
because you were there for mine.

To A.J.

You have a heart of paint.
You leave your mark on people, even when time
has passed, you are still there.
I remember you in a song.
I see you in the wildflowers by my house,
vibrant, happily brightening the landscape.
Missed when the snow comes, but memories can
be just as sweet.
I can't wait to see the paint splatters you leave
on the rest of the world.

To A.L.

What if…
I am sorry for the pain, for yours
and mine.
All those talks, and yet you
and I
never truly got to know one another.
We created a fairytale with different characters
but called them us.
…that question always ends differently.
But after everything, this was never going to end
with Happily Ever After.

To M.M.

Thank you for proving me wrong.
Some walls should crumble.
Cracks can be filled with gold, and something
more beautiful can emerge.
Picking up the shards does not mean accepting
failure but a chance to finally
let   go.
I opened the door, but thank you for giving me
the key.
I think this will be the end of our story, so as a
goodbye, just let me say:
thank you for proving me wrong.

To H.H.L.

3…
This dim house of mirrors taunts me. As soon as I think I've found you, you turn into an empty reflection. Only a mirage of lost hope.
2…
Dead eyes look up, cold and blind. Those can't be yours.
1…
Intricate masks and faces become interchangeable in this dim house of mirrors.
Ready or not, here I come...
Thank you for being the one who made me stop playing hide n' seek with myself.

To M.

You're the weeping willow.
The jungle of roots spread until each leaf gets
what it needs.
You're the redwood.
There will always be a place for you here.
You're the oak.
Standing tall, you continue to inspire.
You are the home that gave during droughts and
floods.

To P.H.

You seem to be able to make gardens grow with
words.
Daisies turned into lifeblood.
Its petals creating a needle to sew together the
rest of my pieces with golden string.
Weeds never stood a chance in your flourishing
garden
where blazing stars, begonias, and bluebells
bloomed.
Thank you for showing me how to start tending
my own.
I will cherish your white roses.

To B.M. & D.

Blood is thicker than water, but water flows
easier.
It purifies and gives life.
You've been a shadow in the back of my mind.
When you grow, guilt quickly leaks through.
There is no blame - just an
emptiness.
They filled it to the brim with a koi fish pond.

To S.C.

You are
f
 a
   l
  l
    i
  n
g.
This isn't the first time, and it won't be the last.
However, there is an art to it.
After the initial terror comes
w e i g h t l e s s n e s s
You will break, but you will also pick up the
pieces.
And aren't new beginnings the most beautiful
thing?